AGE OF EXPLORATION

POEMS BY
CHRISTOPHER SEID

BLUE LIGHT PRESS ◆ 1ST WORLD PUBLISHING

SAN FRANCISCO ◆ FAIRFIELD ◆ DELHI

WINNER OF THE 2015 BLUE LIGHT BOOK AWARD
AGE OF EXPLORATION

Copyright © 2015 by Christopher Seid

All rights reserved. Printed in the United States of America. No part of this book may be used or reproduced in any manner whatsoever without written permission except in the case of brief quotations embodied in critical articles and reviews. For information contact:

1ST WORLD LIBRARY
PO Box 2211
Fairfield, Iowa 52556
www.1stworldpublishing.com

BLUE LIGHT PRESS
www.bluelightpress.com
Email: bluelightpress@aol.com

BOOK & COVER DESIGN
Melanie Gendron

COVER PHOTO
Christopher Seid

AUTHOR PHOTOGRAPH
Ava Grace

FIRST EDITION

Library of Congress Control Number: 2015935037

ISBN 9781421837239

Praise for *Age of Exploration,* Poems by Christopher Seid

Like many of Christopher Seid's friends and fans, I've been waiting for this book for many years. *The Age of Exploration* is full of passion, wonder, mystery and joy – the kind of writing that makes you feel happy to be alive and part of it all. Walk with these poems, "through huckleberry over dunes to Nauset Beach." Gaze at the midnight sky, "Blue ash / from the full moon's burn." "Celestial fireworks." You'll find "Radiant knowledge," luminous moments of angst, like a hitchhiker, "waiting / for someone, anyone, to take him home." At the core of these poems is a quiet transcendence – "Every cell pumped with light." A lingering "'Ah' – drop / of ink in the ocean at night." "Singing *a capella* / some improvisational ode to joy."

—Diane Frank, Author of *Swan Light* and *Yoga of the Impossible*

In *Age of Exploration*, Christopher Seid has crafted a book for seekers, a collection full of questions small and large and journeys far and wide. We encounter a young woman on a late night train on her way to becoming a nun, a young girl in a cornfield in winter, and God as a middle-aged professional woman in heels. "How far are your stars," one poem asks, and "Where's home now that it's too dark to see," asks another. The answers Seid gives come "through mud / and broken bones of last autumn's corn" and a father's fist that's like peony petals packed in a bud. It's these poems lovely images and turns that keep us, along with the poet, like a "quiet passenger, holding on."

—Gibson Fay-Leblanc, Author of *Death of a Ventriloquist*

The poems in Christopher Seid's *Age of Exploration* are important to me not just because they are the recorded history of familiar territory, of places I too have lived, but more because they reveal the stunning transformations of real geography versus the geography of the mind, the heart, and memory: the former prairie towns flooded by reservoirs; the small town schools and cinemas left to the rot of time; the friendships that—though their actors may have died—somehow, miraculously, stay alive, intact, and who, to paraphrase Chris, retrace their steps through darkness to find the place they last stood—to pick up their partner again, position, and the beat.

 — Rustin Larson, Author of *Bum Cantos, Winter Jazz, & the Collected Discography of Morning*

In *Age of Exploration* Christopher Seid gathers memories like salvage, and through them seeks the ever-moving target of truth. These poems exist in a force field between wholeness and limitation, between the longing for transcendence and the realities of responsibility and loss. "What am I supposed to want?" the speaker asks in one poem, and indeed this book considers that crucial question through many brilliant facets of experience. Seid has a real gift for observation, whether he's walking through city streets or rural landscapes. It's a gift for *seeing*, and against what disappears, seeing what remains in "the fading but ever-present & ongoing..."

 —Betsy Scholl, Author of *Otherwise Unseeable*

ACKNOWLEDGMENTS

Thanks to the following magazines and anthologies in which several of these poems first appeared. *Café Review*, "Cape Cod: A Death," "Skiing the Old Farm at Night;" *Maine Magazine:* "Morning Poem;" *River of Earth and Sky: Poems for the 21st Century*: "Age of Discovery," "Hitchhiker," "Full Moon Over Baghdad; March 19, 2003."

The author wishes to thank the following individuals for their suggestions, advice and support over the years these poems were written: Diane Frank, Rustin Larson, Gibson Fay-Leblanc, Betsy Sholl, Tim Kercher, Terry Thaxton, Jim Perry, Paul Knoll and Judy Foster.

I am especially grateful to Mark Johnson—for his friendship, encouragement and close reading of the poems and manuscript.

This book is a creative act. Any resemblance to persons living or dead or to actual incidents or events is purely coincidental.

For my children, Luca & Ava

I know this isn't much.
But I wanted to explain this life to you, even if
I had to become, over the years, someone else to do it.
—Larry Levis

CONTENTS

The Seeker

Cape Cod: A Death...1
Bird Hunting..2
Skiing the Old Farm at Night...3
Hitchhiker..4
The Seeker...5
Long Distance..9
Return to the Place of a Poem...10
Big Bang...12
Age of Exploration...13

Recorded History

Recorded History: Avon Cemetery; Central Iowa; 1998......17
Peonies...21
Grace..22
Working the Scythe...24
Origins...25
Funeral in the Alps..26
Lives of the Poets..27
Falling Tide; Portland, Maine...29
End of the Year..30

The Happy Couple

Morning Poem..33
Italian Wedding...34
Sketches of Spain..36
The Happy Couple..39
Tavern Days, Van Cortland Manor..............................40
The Man in the Coffee Shop Tonight, the One.........41
Ava Grace..43
Flying Home to New England in December..............45

Tranquility Base

Never Coming Home..49
Full Moon Over Baghdad...50
This Madness America...51
PTSD..52
Aneurysm: Near Death Experience............................53
Runaway..54
Leaving New York City...55
What Will Become of Them, This Happy..................57
Tranquility Base...59

Notes..61

About the Author...63

The Seeker

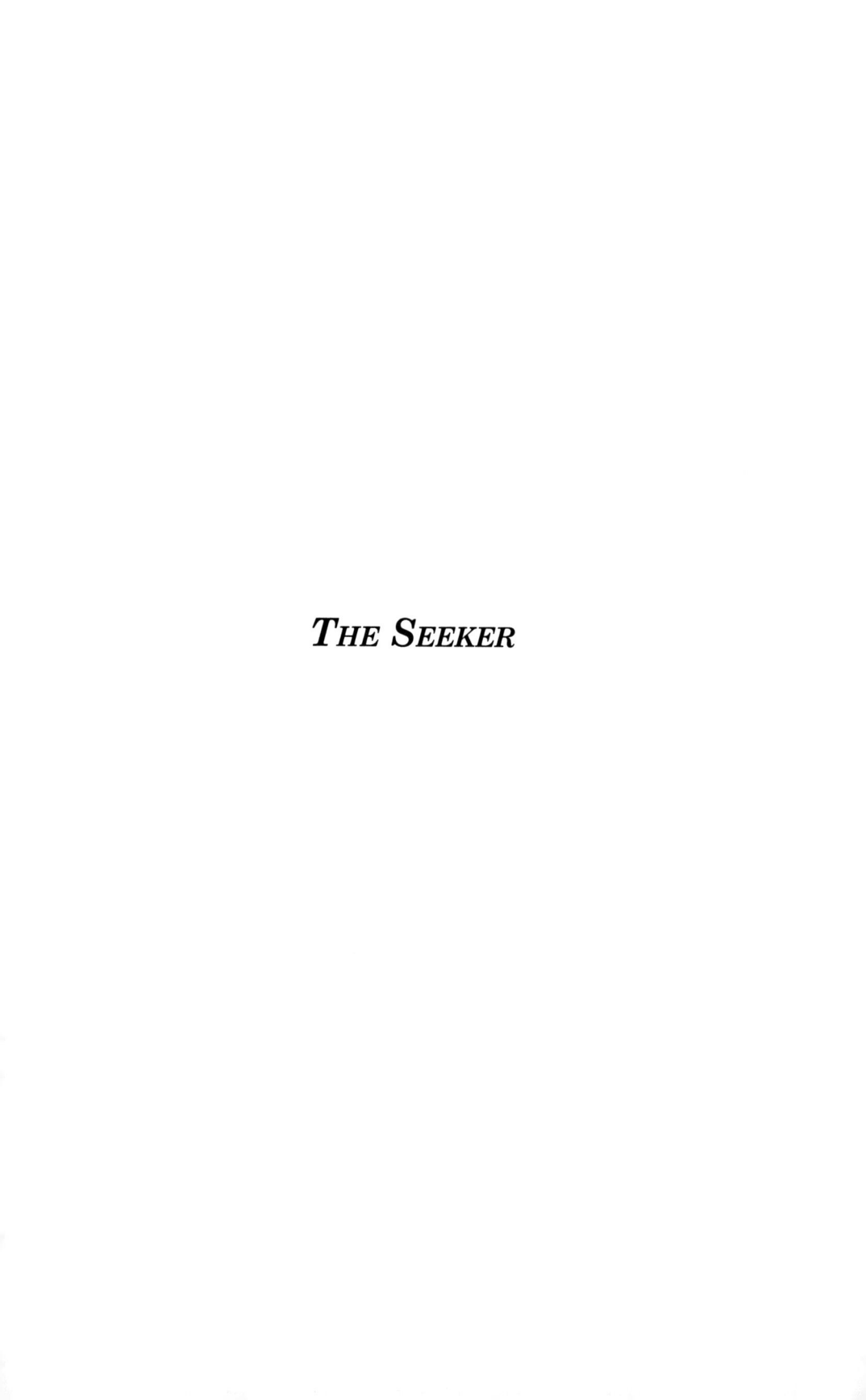

CAPE COD: A DEATH

Tonight, my friend reads Swift to her grandmother,
who's satisfying her final wish to die at home.
The old woman sleeps most of the day, awake nights—
ever since the young doctor explained, *death is like sleep.*

Her breaths are long and studied; she savors each one,
as if she knew how few remained.
I lean in the doorway of the bedroom listening
to soft voices over mechanical pumps and beeps.

I have nothing to do but read, wait, walk quietly about
a house that hoards the residue of late autumn light
like sand or salt inside a translucent shell.
Earlier today, I waded through huckleberry over dunes

to Nauset Beach, where a West African freighter
ran aground in last night's force-nine gale.
Flat to the beach, she settled and creaked, moored to shore
with yellow rope by the local volunteer fire department.

It reminded me of an illustration from *Gulliver's Travels*—
Lilliputians had bound their giant prize
with the burliest cables, and when he awoke, sewn
to the coast of a foreign country, couldn't budge.

The tide ebbed and flowed around the ship's hollow hull,
with the sound inside a shell when pressed to your ear.
When I learned from the crowd that one of its young sailors
was missing, swept overboard in the midnight storm,

I wanted his death to be as easy as sleep—or believe
he might still be found, smoking a cigarette
in his bunk below deck, listening to the old recordings
of Billie Holiday, Duke Ellington and Satchmo

his father had salvaged from before the revolution.

BIRD HUNTING

At the far end of the field, Black Angus
turn slick muzzles to a south wind.

I follow my father's tracks through mud
and broken bones of last autumn's corn

burnished silver in cold. Nothing to hunt
and dusk already, I aim at clouds' ripe

under bellies—the blue-black color of
eggplant, no longer hatching snow.

What I shoot gets away—even sluggish
crows, too quick for my unpracticed eye.

Where's home now that it's too dark to see?

SKIING THE OLD FARM AT NIGHT

The ruts from my two skis
   fill with shadow, blue ash
from the full moon's burn.
   The dogs run ahead

to wrestle ghost dogs
   or a fallen pine bough
shivering in a crooked break.
   I'm panting from the work

of circling this field, nose
   runny and lungs scratched
raw from a head cold. Still,
   it feels good to get close

to the hibernating world,
   to glimpse at least part of
the paralysis underneath.
   I never feel alone here, skiing

beside these trees; I know
   I'm being watched from inside—
good friend gliding with me,
   quiet passenger holding on.

HITCHHIKER

All it takes is watching a ragged crow
   cross a white sky over a snowy field
to inject his heart with a serum of ache.

From the gravel shoulder, he sees nothing
   but a world of gray scale—like stills from
the film *Stranger Than Paradise*—waiting

for someone, anyone, to take him home.
   Silence, yes, but more so, stasis: each
object pressed between time & space,

Reality no thicker than a layer of stain
   or polyurethane. He is a luminous boy
riding around in a pliable exoskeleton—

rubbery to touch, animated, like a light bulb
   stuck inside a polymer puppet. How
did he get here? From what dim smoke

& smolder filled truck cab did he rise
   this morning, into the dome light,
poked awake by the driver's cough

& kicked out into a sleet storm burning
   like buckshot at the edge of Route 34
between Fairfield & Mt. Pleasant, Iowa?

What did that crow & its shadow do
   to rip open in him & reveal the radiance
of being the last living boy on earth?

THE SEEKER

i. My mother's tears reflected in the silver screen

My mother & I watch the final scenes: the hero
leaning from a Moscow streetcar
calls to the beautiful woman he loves.
She doesn't hear him, doesn't turn, but weaves
into the crowd's dense swirl & disappears.
I imagine he whispered her name: *Anna*—
& chasing it through brick streets,
it came to rest on his lips, as he died, like a frozen
six-pointed star.

Five or six years old, & towed by my mother
through the theater's busy lobby at the end of the show,
I asked her: *Is there anyone who knows everything?*
I wanted to find this person, to ask—
*What happens when you die? Where do you go,
& what if you die before you live your life?*
My mother replied: *Nobody knows everything, dear.
It's impossible.*
For the first time in my life I didn't believe her.

ii. The lazy man's guide to enlightenment

As a teenager, I wanted transcendence, escape
from my limitations—choosing early enrollment
in the university of substance abuse.

"Bliss," I read in the *Upanishads*, picked at random
from the stacks during detention,
"is the goal of all sentient beings."

From then on, Truth was the destination
beyond the veil to which I was sentenced to seek—
its celestial fireworks, 24 hours a day.

iii. There was a time when I followed a seer

Growing up in the suburbs of America,
in a large white house with a two-car garage
crammed with more stuff than I could ever use—*what,*
I asked myself, *am I supposed to want?*

It was after midnight when I left the party
to drift alone through summerwoods.
I was probably high or entranced by the face
of my older brother's girlfriend—
because in those days I believed that to be loved
I needed to demonstrate my differences.
So I left, unannounced, without a *thanks* or *see ya,*
to lose myself a thousand miles away
in southern New Hampshire, on a mountain road
oiled & double-dark, vaulted with colossal pines.

Slowly, the cacophonic orchestra
of my family & friends' consternation decayed,
& I followed the tunnel of trees to the end.
That's where I found him, in a clearing, on a pitch
of grass twirling a rose, his calm countenance doused
in a phosphorescent cloud of summer stars.

iv. How to meditate

To begin, sit comfortably
& roll one or two meaningless syllables
on your tongue
like a lozenge of honey & cardamom—
sticky thought dissolving,
effervescent tingle
in your temples & extremities,
every cell pumped with light
until the final dissolution—
breath escaping from a balloon,

& you fading—no pulse, no thought, no name—
into a final smile & lingering "*Ahhh*"—
drop of ink in the ocean at night.

v. Samsaras

Your surprise looked back on itself,
when you were 19, & could almost hear it sigh
& say *goodbye*. Your shudder

in the dark farmhouse at 3 a.m. was final.
Like a child waking from a nightmare—
it wasn't fear, but the bump of the aluminum

boat onto sand, after gliding years through fog.
Visualize: electricity crackling in a tiny wire,
claws of an insect being sharpened at prayer.

It touched you & in the snap
saved you from the ritual drowning. But oh,
how you've been saved so many times since—

each time laid out naked to the point of closing
your eyes, to note another blue anchor etched
on your bicep or a rose on your thigh.

vi. Up in the Grand Hotel, Leysin, Switzerland

This morning I wake from three days of fever & fasting,
to the tolling of a hundred bells—cows
under my window, staggering uphill
along black asphalt, to graze in vivid summer slopes.
They rise through fog & pines, translucent, fading
in & out, like soldiers in camouflage.
A chill mist saturates the air & concrete
I press my naked feet to—but I can't feel it.

I've awakened a different man from the one
who went to sleep the night before—
unfamiliar face in the morning mirror.
Alone, I take a new position: crossed ankles, heel
of my right hand bearing the entirety of my corpse weight
against the cold balustrade.
A mountain thermal strafes my bones
as it blows through a conifer stand.
My skull fills with the perfumed herbs, incense
& aromatic resins reserved for the kings of Babylonia.

vii. Hiking an old logging trail in rain

Above the village of Temple, New Hampshire,
I stop to watch a raven hover over pines—bold
calligraphic *V* on decomposing pages.
Pinned there a moment & shaking out sleep,
it cries three indelible consonants,
before falling through treetops
like a woman's black nylon will fall
from a clothesline into a dew-soaked lawn.

Scrambling off the road then, I let my own
enormous wings unfurl, haul me through that cathedral
of trees, over fragrant floorboards of earth.

LONG DISTANCE

On the phone tonight,
   conviction was absent,
though what you shared
   never suggested why.

It's hard to explain, I know—
   good intentions flail
at the whims of those
   who care little or nothing

for what you aspire: quiet,
   grace, an easy life beside
the lake. Golden winds blow
   blue, from west to east;

the great skin of water
   shivers, green. I'm not
clairvoyant, but I'd guess
   there's something big

you'd rather not discuss,
   in the way you slammed
certain syllables in words
   because and *whatever*;

like a stick being snapped
   by a boot in the woods
at night—the intruder, your
   pain.

RETURN TO THE PLACE OF A POEM

In my old '68 Toyota Corona—barely
an engine, tires and stick shift then—
I crisscrossed county roads north

of Fairfield, Iowa, teaching Shelley
how to drive. Late spring, an exposition
of variations on the color green

framed by roads of incandescent gravel—
stones big as ice cubes knocking holes
in the rusty chassis. Sometimes

we'd stop in the middle of a lake
of clover, no farms or silos in sight,
and make-out on the hood—my hands

chasing hers around our supple selves.
Or we'd coax fistfuls of ditch grass
into the muzzles of starved, listless heifers.

Three years later, living in Cambridge,
Massachusetts, I got word late one night
that Shelley was killed in a collision

on a stretch of wasted Arizona highway.
Winter, New England locked in its heirloom
trunk of ice—and me without key or

combination. Still, sparrows survived,
bickering among twigs of wild grape
that grew under my window.

I was amazed how those birds thrived,
naked at the bottom of bitter cold—
proving just how difficult it is to die.

Yet, when it happens to someone
so young, I wonder if it isn't meant to be:
Shelley just wanted to dance, but the palsy

she was born with carried her feet
in the opposite direction
from where she intended to go. I knew

spring would return in a few months
and green reclaim the city and suburbs.
So, I asked, why shouldn't we? Retracing

our steps through darkness to find
the place we'd last stood—to pick up
our partner again, position, and the beat.

BIG BANG

There's something terrifying
   out there, something frail—
      a river bone no bigger than

an acorn, a bouquet
   of weed flowers, long bloomed
      & gone to seed—now

a smudge of dust, ash.
   This, what disappears—
      sloughed-off skin, hair, nails,

the blood & bone of being.
   What remains is the fading
      ever-present & ongoing

boom of the primordial *Idea*
   that fueled & stoked this mass,
      mess. Nothing but rubble

of ideas now, cracked &
   cracking into invisible rabble—
      elements, molecules, atoms.

As time continues, will it slow
   & stall? Will the wreckage
      of what remains thicken

to eternity? Or will it dissipate
   into a stoned quiet, everything
      deaf & stumbling through

the density of *silencio supremo*?

AGE OF EXPLORATION

It was a shining moment that day
I discovered coffee in college. Finally,
something legal to keep me focused
on Kierkegaard and Proust,
or interjecting opinions
into a midnight dorm debate
over punk versus grunge.
Sometimes, I'd leave the books butterflied
on my bed at 3 a.m.
and walk through campus alone—
Midwest air sticky with aromas
of plowed earth and cows.
I continued this ritual long after I graduated
and moved to New York City;
23 and on my own, I was free to wander
hot city streets till dawn.
The coffee kept me going and, one night,
coming back late to my apartment
in Park Slope, high on shots
of double espresso and *Gauloises*,
felt my brain crackle with pure consciousness
as I fumbled for the key, singing *a cappella*
some improvisational ode to joy.
I wasn't returning to anyone or anything;
I could do whatever I wanted, go
wherever I pleased.
So I went home, lit a candle, and opened a book
—Ovid's *Metamorphosis*—
to read the story of Orpheus and Eurydice.
Years later, after my divorce,
I was on a train blasting through Nebraska's
Western sand hills
when I cracked that book again.
Hot wind blew straight from the sun
as I drank coffee in the smoking car

with an old woman from Chicago.
She must be dead now—at the time,
halfway Hades with emphysema.
I remember she kept the car awake all night
coughing so convulsively I thought she'd choke—
while her devoted husband
shuffled to and from the bathroom
for towels and cool water.
All I could do was read about love
and the risks of blind devotion,
when my eyes lit upon the face of a girl
sitting across from me.
Only 18, she was on her way to work
in a nunnery that summer,
because she was thinking of joining *The Order*.
I might have tried talking her out of it,
describing, with perhaps too much zeal,
the pleasures of—what—*Love? Romance? Sex?*
I didn't say it, but thought
she might get the idea from the story
of Orpheus and Eurydice I shared.
While I never knew for sure,
she did accept my offer
to buy her a cup of coffee, her first,
and recommendation to take it black.
Although it was weak, brewed
from cheap Amtrak grounds,
the caffeine took hold and she spoke for hours
about the love of her life: Jesus Christ.
And for a long time during our ride together,
through the middle of night, middle
of nowhere, I also believed.

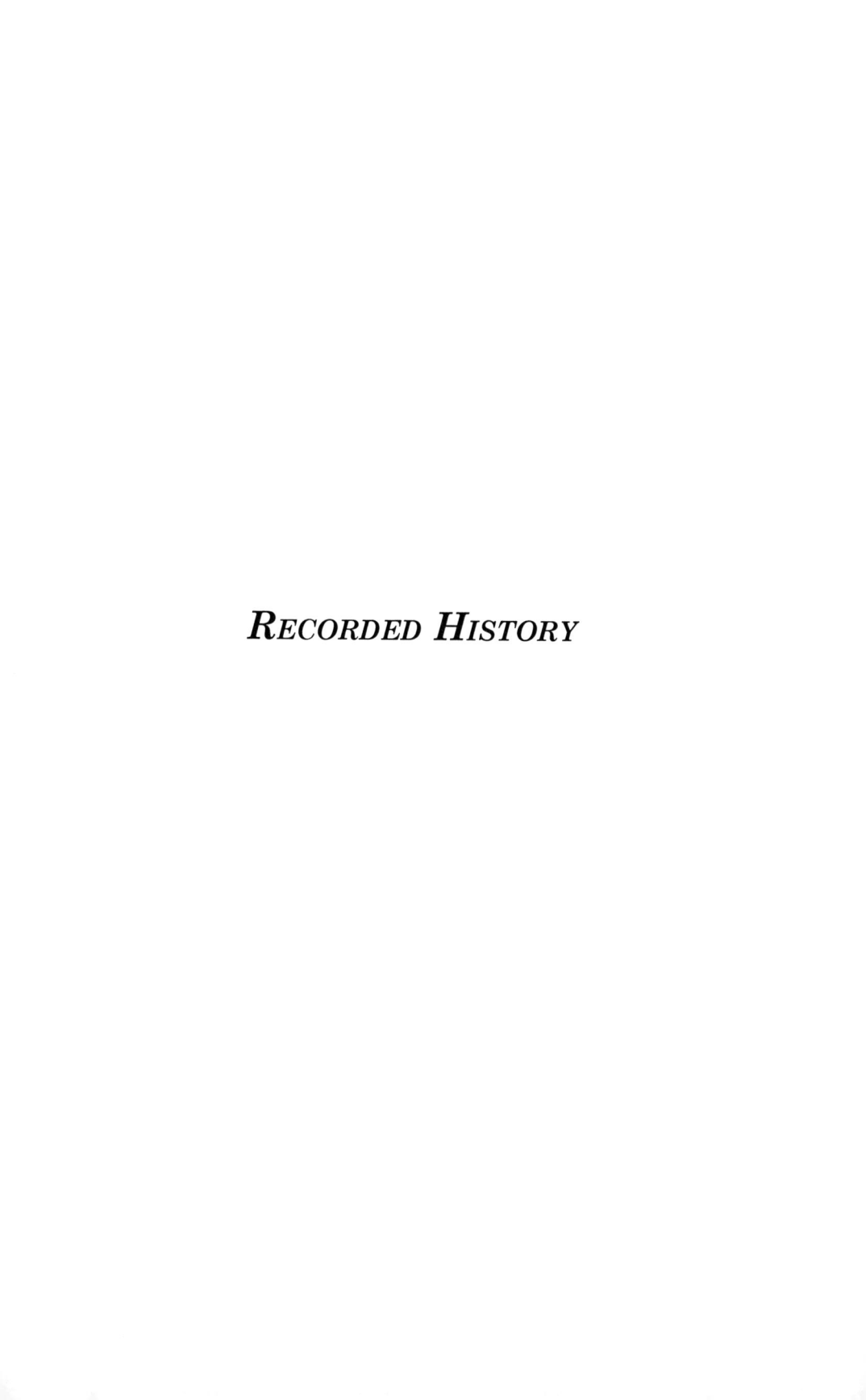

RECORDED HISTORY

RECORDED HISTORY:
AVON CEMETERY; CENTRAL IOWA, 1998

How can a man, born April 1, 1900, expect to laugh
at the joke, much less survive, 98 years of the 20th Century?
His birthday, marked by a shaft of rebar pounded three feet
into Iowa topsoil. Slowly the earth around it erodes;
the post begins to rust, rot, lean and become lost
in bramble—thistle, cocklebur, bittersweet—
in a neglected corner of cornfield, Middle America.

> *'Course my dad's mother and father is buried here.*
> *Like I say, there was seven or eight in the family:*
> *William, Anna, John, Jake, Charlie, my dad and the*
> *twins.*
> *And my older sister is buried right over there.*
> *Stillborn; never was a marker there.*

Every year a technological advance, equal in power and scope
to the atomic bomb, carves a new blemish on the century's profile.
But it happens without notice; the mind's tricked
into calling it "progress"—like the pot of water raised slowly
to the boiling point, in which the contented, oblivious frog
reclines. I see a sleek new factory spewing soot.
I see a nuclear warhead aimed at the dark side of the moon.

> *My dad never did talk about his youth growing up*
> *in the old country. He was seven years old*
> *when he come over here. He had one brother and three*
> *sisters: Amelia, Henry, August—who married*
> *Charlie Aurbach—and Ireka, the youngest.*

I see a landscape with a footprint wide as a superhighway.
I see the little town where he grew up—underwater now,
a recreational reservoir surrounded by split-level homes.
There's nothing left of the farms he worked; the mule teams
he hitched to drive out of the coal mine are dust.

The hayfields, the pretty girls he flirted with, the photographer
who caught him in 1917 atop the haywagon, arms akimbo.

> *Ireka was married seven or eight times.*
> *And one of her husbands tried to cut her throat.*
> *Damn near got the job done! She had two sons*
> *with Charlie Ewald. Ward, they called him Skinny.*
> *And Ludwig, they called him Sliver.*

Along this smoky gravel road it rains ice through big
sycamores and cottonwoods. Nearly deaf, Clarence talks
as if submerged in those days—in fragrance of cut hay
and horse manure baking in a humid June field.
I am the scribe, driving the ghost of the old bard, Ovid,
around his ancestral home outside Rome—Augustus dead—
after a 30-year exile in Tomis, near the Black Sea.

> *Uncle Charlie was a bricklayer, and a damn good one.*
> *He kinda went berserk, I don't know what . . .*
> *They had him in the bughouse out in the county farm.*
> *Before you know it, he was on the outside layin' brick.*
> *He was 99 or a hundred when the old fart died.*

We pass the one-room schoolhouse, used now for town storage,
where Clarence wept under the stars, 1912, after losing
the spelling bee. The word: *appendicitis.* Here, the same
vast cornfields in which he'd play, ghostly stalks now,
interrupted by cottonwoods along one of the thousand creeks
that feed the Raccoon River. He reminds me of his many fishing
expeditions, casting for bullheads and "log-layin'" walleyes.

> *Out there was a potter's field. The only one I ever knew*
> *buried there was an old Civil War soldier named*
> *Maynard.*
> *Son of a bitch yelled at me once for wasting well water.*
> *That's the old church there. When I was young the first one*
> *burnt down. The second one burnt down. This one hasn't*
> *burnt down.*

Time is a movie screen. Those years—1910 through 1915—
project in the windshield as we drive. They live—flesh, breath, bodies
in a crowded carnival, colored lights, music, horse barns
and hay, straw hats and ladies' colorful parasols spinning.
He asks me to stop, to watch sooty-faced mineworkers
march mule wagons into daylight of humid summer noon.
He speaks to each one—recites their names—all dead.

> *My granddad died over where that pond is.*
> *It's the entrance to the mineshaft. Or it was.*
> *Full of water now. He went down to get a bucket*
> *to water his cows and never come up.*
> *Killed by the black damps. Hell, I was just a kid . . .*

April wind flings soil in our faces from rows of disced fields;
no trees to slow the cold blast down from the Dakotas.
We walk the family plot at Avon cemetery, where names
carved into white stones have been erased by years of weather,
like brand names stamped in bars of half-used soap.
Clarence isn't bothered, but I button my coat to the neck.
We stop before a row of his clan—fathers, mothers, sisters, cousins...

> *Uncle John was a strange bird. Killed himself drinking*
> *carbolic acid. It's a lousy way to go.*
> *Seemed his girlfriend fell for another guy.*
> *Ol' John wrote her nasty letters then signed*
> *the other feller's name. The letters got traced to him.*

World War I. The Crash and Depression. WW II...
He stares out the window as the boys march home from field
work, rakes and scythes slung over shoulders like shotguns.
We pass the little shack by the rusty tracks—Raccoon Valley—
where at night he'd raise a burning newspaper
to stop a freight train, take a 12-cent ride to downtown
Des Moines, the burlesque show at the Princess Theater.

This used to be a big vineyard in here, you know.
Owned by Red Brooks. He was shyster; done very well.
He's a good guy. But he was a sucker. He was what
you call a card sharper. Look at that orchard. I think
there used to be another airshaft to the mine around
here...

It was called Coal Hill, and once hummed like an ant colony.
In a landscape by Grant Wood, farmers drive teams
of horses over rectangles of espresso-black earth,
or miners swarm the entrance to the shaft at their shift change.
Children slam screen doors and scamper out to converge
on a country road for the long walk to school.
A hundred feet below, burly men whack picks into soft rock.

I remember ol' Everett. Used to plug maple trees
with tobacco. There's one over there. He'd punch leaves
in the holes in the trees and let it set there all winter.
That's how he'd get his chewin' tobacco. Tobacco grows
good in this country. Trouble is it grows too rank.

Like the burning of the Great Library of Alexandria, every
old person takes an epoch to the grave—impressions
and memories, to smoke and ash and earth.
Before he dies, Clarence hands off to me his favorite
pocketknife and chrome harmonica, bundled in the red bandana
he always carried. What will I do with these, I ask—
I don't whittle and I don't blow?

Used to be a brick-making factory down there.
Under the reservoir now. Every house made of brick.
Knew a family that lived in one of 'em. One of the girls
taught piano. She used to drive out to give me lessons.
Rose, I think her name was; Rose Miller.

PEONIES

My father's peonies, blooms heavy and white as new baseballs,
hover in shadow on the south side of our house.
He stands over them at the end of his workday, smoking, filling
the little moats he's dug around each stalk with city water
from a green hose. I can hear water slapping mud.
In the back yard, heirloom roses, eggplant, tomatoes, a few herbs.
My father pampers these, his pet projects, his relaxation technique,
after an impossible week of selling lingerie along back roads
and blacktop. Sometimes, on weekends, he holds the catcher's mitt
while I practice pitches. I imagine his hand inside that oily
leather glove. Is it suffocating in there? Would it rather be holding
a sleek white cigarette? A hose? The steering wheel? A sample case?
The peonies amaze me—how such a fat, fragrant gob of petals
can be packed inside that tiny green knot of a bud.
Like my father's fist.

GRACE

> *By God's grace I'm still alive.*
> —Johnny Cash

The way my brother tells it, he died
answering the doorbell.
The undercover cop pressing the .38's
Cyclopean eye to his forehead

triggered the movie of his life: crude
Super-8s of a celebrated childhood—
conquering the ten-foot snowdrift, or
his teammates swarming the plate

after his solo shot to left.
But just as quickly, the film ends
in a flash (camera pointed toward
the sun) and my brother stopped

breathing—a scream stuck in his throat
like a chicken bone. The next thing
my brother knew, he was cuffed,
belly-down on blue shag, the cop's knee

like a kitchen knife in his scapula.
My brother had time to trace the sequence
of bad choices that dropped him here:
an apartment in a hostile Southern state,

two cops hiding in double-dark,
chrome triggers tense and waiting
for the roommate to arrive—as he did,
right on time, whistling through the door,

a pound of Bolivian blow in his backpack.
My brother prayed, *Dear Jesus, what
kind of fuckhead have I become?* And Christ—
the way my brother tells it—answered

with a calming grip, celestial fingertips
pressing into his skull. One o'clock
in the morning, Christmas Eve,
he tells me this story—hands flying

on the back of swift adrenalin—
swearing once more
upon his witness. I've heard him tell it
before, and every time his eyes close

at the part where Jesus enters
his heart, tongue caught
in a kind of chocolate bliss.
Though it has been over two years

since he was saved, to tell it
refuels his faith and lust to believe
in the supernatural, the inexplicable
mystery to which he clings

like ocean flotsam. At the county jail
he bargained his way to 10 days,
his landlady accepting bail—
the one condition he attend church

with her. Now, his crucifix swings
from his neck like a pendulum, seconds
ticking away the hours, days
to when he joins his Lord in Paradise.

WORKING THE SCYTHE

I begin on wild roses, tentacled to stone walls;
    blossoms pink and white, divided with a swipe.

The air's interrogated with scents of dollar perfumes,
    while thistle, smartweed, goldenrod are tipped

to rest like wind-blown vases on graves.
    I don't think, just sway, lost in the body's rhythm

of joint and muscle, clattering rake of bones—my heart
    tapping out meter, weight and aim of measured swaths.

What music the blade and stem release—sonorous ring—
    not apology or warning, a key indifferent to the end?

All afternoon it sings—clipping foxtail, wild iris
    and Queen Anne's lace at the knees—

grouse doom, wrecked homes of butterfly and snake.
    If I miss, clip a rock or stump, rack the edge rough,

I'll peen and whet it clean again—stone's course tongue
    along the quarter-moon curve.

My strokes start slow, slipping away off the blade—
    but soon scratch faster, a few sparks fly.

ORIGINS

Grub infested logs, halfway to loam
from rot & redundant boot steps.

Humid nights, pockets of clotted heat—
mosquitos' pinprick, warbling frogs,

dark scent of molder & eyes.
Crouch beside the surface

membrane—toad spawn leak
from burbling perimeters—

& witness life congeal, mass
of biology organizing

into innate patterns, deliberate cells.
Cell-to-cell, something new

circulates, penetrates—an urge
rising, & from it, a snarl.

First thought, then sight, thump—
a primordial hand reaching for food.

FUNERAL IN THE ALPS

Blue deluge, soaking sting
  of pine & layers
    of smoldering snow.

The one rare, pink lady
  slipper she reached for
    under a conifer

at the edge of the granite
  crevasse. Why, he asked,
    must you have that one?

To press in your hand, she
  said, like a prism made
    of God's glass.

LIVES OF THE POETS

Driving 16 hours straight, determined
to make it all the way in one day,
you mistake the rising full moon
for a neon sign, an oil company's familiar logo.

It startles you the way your father's face did,
when you woke at 5 a.m.
to find him rocking in the chair beside your bed.
He hadn't slept all weekend, and you wondered

if his countenance was imitating the moon's—astonished,
a hole in his face the size of Dakota—
now that his wife, your mother, was gone.
Turning off the rock and roll CD, something raucous

but smart—the 'Mat's *Pleased to Meet Me*—
you enter silence, a region that makes you suspicious,
and in which you've never been comfortable.
In the rearview mirror, your father is standing in the driveway

waving goodbye. You wonder why you didn't cry at her funeral,
if it matters or not. All you know is, you're tired,
and how easy it would be to coax the Toyota into a rest stop,
cut the engine and sleep till dawn.

Sitting up late in the kitchen of my Brooklyn apartment,
I'm guessing you're somewhere between Minneapolis
and Virginia, crossing flat Ohio,
your head raging with quarrels that feed great art.

At my window, the same full moon struggles to clear a fence
of the public school across Court Street—
its pitted face and orange pallor magnified
by a thick lens of humidity and polluted air.

I tap my pencil on the rim of a ceramic mug
with a large leaf pattern repeating over a pastel blue underglaze
that reminds me of palm trees against a sunset in LA,
where I lived when you and Susan came to visit.

Remember, one evening, how the sun setting in front of us
reflected high clouds that slid
like tie-dyed cotton above a kaleidoscopic sea, not thundering?
Susan and I called you to come out onto the patio to look,

but you were deep inside the guestroom,
blinds dropped against the distracting sun and sea,
writing a story about the night you were busted tagging
the bricks outside your high school gymnasium.

The authorities plastered your picture all over local news,
embarrassing your devoted parents.
It was a fluke; you were no delinquent—the one stupid dare
you'd ever made good on.

But there, on the patio, facing that beautiful ocean vista,
all you could say was *harrumph!*—so unlike the stories you write,
that reach for and achieve high empathy and elegy.
Going back to work, you stayed in that room all night, alone—

Susan and I eating dinner in silence without you.

FALLING TIDE, PORTLAND, MAINE

Gulls overhead, dumpling-sized & dreaming
in a blue velvet sky,
are double exposed in broken-brick pools
of cool, kaleidoscopic water.

The angler's taut thread, a superficial flaw
against the drawbridge imposing.
Now, suppose a cosmos diorama: cranked
flywheel of creation—spray of sparks, cinders

going dark & hiss into seawater; waves
like nets flung, & tethered to them
clumps of breathing bodies.
Silent stop-time explosions, jittery & slick,

spangle of sea glass, suds, trash—everything
coming out of nothing, in threes, & returning.

END OF THE YEAR

> *The air is a smear of ash*
> *with the cool taste of coins.*
>   —Anthony Hecht

Freshets of golden chill; shifting, sighing leaves.
Darker greens nod. Flowers' final colors, fading, dry.
If a dog barks, or a child cries, or a woman's footsteps
quicken in gravel under your window,
you know it's only the residue of a dream (the dreamer
awakened by the choke of wood smoke and ash).
And lights go out. And doors slam and lock.
And winter settles in with the intense focus
of a foreign student. And fires get stoked to roar.
And every rodent cowers in its knot, nest or burrow.
And you wake in the middle of the night
to walk your house in a robe—barefoot on cold floorboards—
thoughtless, tired, out of shape and out of breath,
from scrambling uphill for all you've ever wanted.

THE HAPPY COUPLE

MORNING POEM

I'm not the kind of
   lover you'd expect:
reclusive rain-
   walker, late sleeper
and lingerer into a
   too long night.

You are the other
   hand: early beautiful,
worthy of flurry
   and applause from
red-winged flocks raiding
   each sunrise.

ITALIAN WEDDING

1.

The night before his wedding,
the groom sits in a Pittsburgh hotel room
sick with a head cold.
He just wants to sleep—or stand in a hot shower,
then freeze in front of an open window.

October, and the young man's exhausted.
What he remembers is a life alone—long days working
on the orchard, and late nights not thinking.
Now he's staggering along the road after a minor car accident—
blood on his face from a small cut over his eye.

He remembers only what he's insisted on
forgetting: The abstract color of aluminum, blush
of a polished snow bank.
It all comes back to him now—the taste
of a fresh-picked Macintosh: tart
as the word "pectin," unsatisfying as the word "pulp."

2.

Not tonight, O Muse, I have a headache.
My fingers are burned from handling all day the sun.
My forehead's frozen from leaning it all night
against the moon.
Tonight I toast my new friends, death and marriage.
I lapse into a rambling, epic reverie—
and the ambulance comes.
O Muse, you poke my shoulder to wake me,
but I'm too tired to sing, too despondent to ring
the bell that calls the starlings home.
My bones have turned to granite. My skin is mud.
My hair is woven into the oriole's nest.
O Muse, tonight I toast my bride-to-be, across town,

sleeping in her own bed for the last night.
Let me guzzle my drink and slip out, walk alone
the black streets of this grand old iron town.
Tomorrow morning is a hundred years away.
Let me wake to drizzle and an hour
luminous in the future: I see a white globe
with a skull painted on it.
Or is it the porthole of our ghost ship
covered with a deteriorating lace doily?
I toast the moon, that ancient portal
through which the soul escapes at death.
Then I snap out of it, laughing at my absurd past—
but not without lifting a jar to the alter of youth.
O Muse, will you deliver me whole?
Or will my legacy disintegrate like foam
in the wake of our honeymoon cruise ship?

3.

A gob of smoke—frankincense—spills
onto cold flagstones of the immense Sacred Heart Church.
It crawls like a talon toward the alter.
The small crowd's quiet in the reverberations
of the organ's explosive finale. Rain seeps through
a triangular break in a pane of red stained glass.
The old priest groans on about snows of centuries and sorrows.
Love that is located in the heart of Christ . . .

4.

in medeas res
    mea culpa
        mamma mia!

SKETCHES OF SPAIN

1. *Mallorca*

One hundred centuries of white stones
clattering down from volcanic hills,
click like ice cubes into a cellophane sea.
Tiny parasites, crawling on these hills,
dressed in white shirts and straw hats,
scar it with chisels and iron plows.
They gather stones like grains of rice
and build walls, villages, cities;
they plant ten million olive trees
like sutures in red flesh. Sometimes,
the only visible thing for miles
is a single flea riding a scooter.
Here, women in black walk dirt roads
only natives and lost *turistas* know.
They mourn husbands who disappeared
years ago—propped up in dingy bars
and *cervezaterias* from Palma to Cala Ratjada—
dead from having pulled glass triggers
on one too many shots of rot gut rye.

2. *Pamplona*

Trapped in traffic, we scan for a spot to park
near a sunny table where we might rest
with tapas and glasses of cold, tart sidra.
Instead, we're spun around the city's central fountain,
before kicking out beside the bullring
onto Hemingway Lane. It's here they run the bulls in July—
each horned, one-ton catastrophe
bearing down the back of its chosen denizen.
This stadium is like others I've seen throughout Spain:
Moorish arches, brick earth the color of dried blood,
Arabic script curved like drawn sabers.

I take a few choice shots with my Nikon,
glad the street is empty, quiet as a tomb.

3. *Arquillos*

Late summer revelers go quiet,
browsing shop windows glassy-eyed
from wine and lack of sleep.
Even the constable's white horse
is silent—gliding cobblestones
on delicate, gilded hooves.
Dusk comes early, and from its dust
a parade of taillights extinguished
by distant, smoke-colored hills.
We arrived earlier from those hills,
to walk this town's drowsy streets,
beside its distinguished lake
topped-off with shivering, silver water.
Tired from driving all day, we'd rather
assume the disguise of twilight haze
and sleep. But the porch lights
on every cantina expose us—dare us
to enter, take a seat and indulge
in a plate of mama's roast chicken
and bottles of cold, tart sidra.

1. *Donostia-San Sebastian*

Exhausted by the many righteous ways to die,
I leave the cold cathedral in mid-tour
to walk among tan, beautiful bodies locked in love on sand.
I imagine Hemingway went this way,
before crowds of *Americanos* arrived to follow his
infamous zigzag steps. In late summer sun,
I watch grand white masts on the horizon
evaporate into superstitious distances—like conquistadors
who once punctured this veil in grotesque galleons,
inspired by the slaughtered soldiers of Christ: Saint Sebastian,

pin-cushion for pagan arrows;
bones of martyred bishops entombed in flagstones;
locks of hair from ninth century nuns
soldered into stems of ceremonial crosses.
It's no wonder I fear this young man,
who, screaming into a cell phone, charges toward me—
the tails of his black shirt spinning like wings of *el diablo*.

THE HAPPY COUPLE

The only thing they can't talk about is death—
she starts to cry, saying she can't bear the thought
of leaving this life, earth and its private leisures.

So they walk downtown instead, into the lush elements
of street life thriving along Sixth Avenue in the Village—
where sleepwalkers swing down from trapeze heights

and ghosts rise from the West 4th stop, after years
of riding the rickety *Shuttle*. It's here, under a full moon
bloodshot by the grit of concrete and exhaust, he believes

you die—from the grit kicked up by the pace of life, not
the pace alone. While she, on the other hand, tiptoes
so not to step where the homeless have laid out

fragments of their lives to sell: sooty clothes
snagged from dumpsters, used books, ads ripped out
of old issues of *Vanity Fair, Life, Cosmopolitan*.

The couple doesn't say much then, only feel—the frantic
reflections in neon and steel, flesh cornered
in the crosswalk, a flash of headlights like a snapshot

captioned with a rage of tires, horns, four-letter words.

TAVERN DAYS, VAN CORTLAND MANOR, CROTON-ON-HUDSON, NEW YORK

Slowly getting sleepy from tasting
tiny cups of locally brewed ales and IPAs,
I'm nodding in a field of close-cropped zoysia—
my two-year-old son climbing
an empty picnic table just out of reach.
I'm not a reckless parent.
I'm no more looped than a honeybee, who,
stumbling headlong into a virgin buttercup,
pops up gleaming head-to-toe
in golden pollen, and grinning.
It's the Indian Summer sun that's got me pinned—
while a bucket of cold wind off the Hudson
attempts to shock me from my languor.
Forgive me.
All I ask for is one half-day a week
to shut down completely, unplug my consciousness
from the turbines of responsibility
that drive middle age.
I'll be lucky to get a moment's peace
before my son begs me to wrestle or chase him—
his little hand pulling me up off the ground
like the magic tugboat in the children's story he reads,
the one who comes with a winch
to rescue the once great and mighty ocean liner
from the bottom of the sea.

THE MAN IN THE COFFEE HOUSE TONIGHT, THE ONE

drinking espresso and smoking a *Gauloises*, he
is not me. That man at the jazz club,
in the East Village, and later, the one walking
the streets, his arm around a beautiful
young woman—he is not me. Or that man,

at the all-night diner now, talking art, poetry
and music with friends as the place empties and
neon lights buzz louder above the softening traffic
of the West Side Highway—he is not me.
Or that man, back at his apartment, happy,

generous, making love to the woman who loves
him—he is not me. That man, who on Sunday
morning, spreads *The New York Times* on the floor,
with coffee and bagels, reading till noon—he
is not me. No, I am the older man, the one

with flecks of gray in his hair and beard, who
is just getting up from his table, leaving
a generous tip when the younger man arrives
with his date. I am the man who is polite, who
orders decaf, who no longer smokes—even

a popular brand of light cigarette. I am the man
who speaks more of his career and disappointments
than of his wild ambitions and expectations.
I am the man who prefers nostalgic rock, 50s
jazz or acoustic music, who rarely traverses the city

at night, who is home in the suburbs from work
in time to tuck in his children, and who himself
is often in bed and asleep by 10 p.m. That's me,
the man who wakes early to make coffee, check

his email, feed the cat and walk the dog, who prepares

the house before his children tumble out of bed
and down the stairs, to be met by breakfast
he has prepared with love—glasses of juice,
bowls of cereal, plates of toast, eggs and bacon
smiling up at them.

AVA GRACE

In my early 20s, jobless, I was crashing
in a borrowed house on Cape Cod,
when God appeared to me in a dream—
a middle-aged professional woman
in heels, perfume, a blue dress and pearls.

I don't recall much of those days, only
the cinderblock balanced on my chest
that kept me awake nights
on a queen-sized mattress on the floor.
I didn't have an income or the means to fix

my Valiant that blew oil as I drove
Route Six looking for work and friends.
It was the dream that resuscitated me:
I was in a seamless white room
with a few strangers, waiting my turn.

I remember thinking: meeting God
is a once in a lifetime thing;
I should be prepared to ask big questions
about life and death. But when she
approached, all I could do was stutter

petty, self-indulgent worries.
Pressing her index finger to my lips,
she whispered something *sotto voce*
in a foreign tongue I didn't understand.
The next morning, I awoke saturated

with a palpable calmness that remained
for months—whatever she said
put me at ease, like a friend's arm
around my shoulder after an especially
ugly argument. I was feeling confident

and in control of my life for the first time
in years, when I received a job offer in L.A.
So I left the Cape and, after living out west
a few years, moved to New York City
where my life began in earnest: I met

and married a pretty artist from Pittsburgh,
bought a house in Westchester, became
a commuter—pursuing a 15-year career
in advertising. In that time, I've lived
my life, won my share and lost some,

gone gray at the temples, hurt and
disappointed people, made others laugh,
forgotten names and faces, misplaced
important numbers and addresses. And
to those friends and strangers from whom

I've learned, for better or worse,
and to those I've failed to keep up with
and sincerely thank, let me say: I'm forever
grateful. But it wasn't until yesterday,
sitting in a chair beside the public pool,

I remembered my dream of God.
I was watching my three year-old daughter
fill a bucket from the deep-end, splash it
on my feet; she was working hard
in the hot sun, intent on keeping daddy cool.

That's when I understood the words
God whispered 18 years earlier: *Be patient,*
she said, *you'll be fine—one day saved
by a little girl with blond hair and hazel eyes,
your daughter.*

FLYING HOME TO NEW ENGLAND IN DECEMBER

Who sees the rush into dusk
the way a passenger does
from her window seat
on a jetliner heading east?
Who sees clouds assembling
like puzzle pieces below, cracked
and already plowed under?
Who sees a kitchen light
snap on—someone up
from a nap or Steeler game
on TV, clattering in the fridge
for a cold bottle of IC?
Who sees, across town,
last light flare on the forehead
of a boy riding his bike
in the parking lot of the diner,
where his mother is smoking
on the step at her shift's end?
Who sees flurries snag
like dull sequins in her perm,
on the collar of her pink uniform
& nametag: LOUISE—
white type knocked out
on black plastic & pinned
to her breast? Who sees
the silver flash of fuselage
as the plane wheels a few degrees
north, away from teal & deeper
into turquoise—etching its fading,
final contrail? Who sees . . .

TRANQUILITY BASE

NEVER COMING HOME

"Everything is everything . . . but you're missing."
—Bruce Springsteen

You've had the bathroom remodeled and dining room
painted, but nothing freshens your mind, not even this—
the season's first snowfall, hiding everything familiar.
You can still feel the wet mark of his kiss on your cheek

when he left that morning—running out the door, late
for the train. The balloons he blew up for your daughter's
birthday, two day's before, held his breath for weeks.
He never liked working in that building, on the 89th floor,

describing often how, on windy days, it would sway—
doors opening and closing without effort, water sloshing
around in restroom toilets. He often discussed quitting,
and opening his own practice, an office closer to home.

The walk and driveway already need shoveling.
You watch from the kitchen window as your oldest son
begins to scoop and toss. Working hard to fit in chores
between homework and swim team, he nods to you—

but all you see is innocence hardening to a bitter glare.

FULL MOON OVER BAGHDAD; MARCH 19, 2003

White buildings mirrored in the Tigris—
damp air stagnant with derision
and the scent of burgeoning spring.
A child's cry from an upper window,
faint as an insect or distant siren.
The light flicks on. A young mother
crosses the room to investigate.
This was said to have been the cradle
of civilization, where some believe
the Garden of Eden flourished. *Imagine
dense primordial palms, lush
aromatics and hibiscus, redolent fungi
and moss-steeped rain gathering
like silver on broad black leaves.
Deeper in, smolder of a campfire—
evidence of afterglow and a sexual
encounter. Disappearing into brush,
footprints—and further in, a growl.*
The fable interrupted now by advanced
pyrotechnics—not lightning or
fireworks—the under bellies of clouds
lit up by the flash of Howitzers.
Pigeons shaken off rooftop roosts,
settle back into limestone dust.
Palm trees toss shaggy heads and teeter.
Goats shiver in suburban yards
and roosters scatter. On the horizon,
the full moon rises, red as a pomegranate,
aloof and indifferent to the bombing.

THIS MADNESS AMERICA

White horses lug the flag-shrouded coffin of our president
   to his final resting place in the highlands of Arlington.

21 guns explode. An iceberg of smoke floats in. The tide recedes.
   A lone sailboat tacks, seeking entrance to the Chesapeake—

its triangle of nylon like a handkerchief snapping surrender.
   The crowd of 50 million is silent, awaiting word.

A change of guard and no one notices: the last cigar tamped out
   in a crystal ashtray, or the final drop of single malt poured

in the lobby of the Willard Inter Continental. The new president
   leads us in prayer for a speedy recovery, for the smoke to clear,

for the last bullet to rot in our new found land of less—America
   still raging its mad course through naked stars.

PTSD

You wake in the middle of the night
unable to breathe, a divot in your throat
the size of a boot scuff in red sand.

Flash of a stab wound or bullet hole
becomes a widening, bloody crevasse—
shattered skin, skull, complete limbs scattered.

As much as you'd like to, you can't recoil
into a crack or shell, from the shadows
that goose-step under your window, over

stonewalls, through the garden, into your
bedroom and out the back—your limp body
in the arms of another monster dream.

ANEURISM: NEAR DEATH EXPERIENCE

His aorta didn't burst, as it typically will,
but tore instead, and "seeped"—or so the surgeon explained.
They shut down his heart to work on it—blood
detoured like traffic around city construction.
Picture a sever in asphalt, steam hissing up
through a ruptured main.

He slumbered in the OR, in a bathtub of ice,
like a slab of Atlantic salmon prepped and readied for the grill.
After the heart's patched, they jump it with a tickle of electricity.
My father woke slowly—weeks it seemed to take him—
like a bear from hibernation.

Three days I watched the moon wax to full
through the hospital's big picture window, and paced outside,
smoking with the nurses and Latino orderlies.
My father cried when he saw me; he knew he was lucky to be alive.
Within a week he was his old self again—
spitting venom about Democrats and taxes.

RUNAWAY

Naked midriff, ample cleavage exposed
by a pushup and skin-tight leopard print top,
she kisses her *Marlboro Red*, exhaling
from the corner of her thin-lipped mouth.

Her lips, tongue and ears are silver-studded,
hooped, hooked and chained. Her arms
etched with purple *phantasmagoria*.
On the boardwalk, looking for a scrum

with other scruffs picked up along the way,
she's distracted by games—ring toss, balloon,
darts—and toothless barkers begging patrons
to play and lose. Then it's the Ferris wheel,

glittering. Or a pink bouffant, enormous
cupcake of irresistible cotton candy...
Shaking out her hair—green-golden streaks,
like spring leaves on a flimsy bough—

she glances from the boy to whom her arm's
loosely latched. Just watch, any moment now,
when no one's looking, she'll make her getaway—
slipping between booths to lose the crowd

and set off alone into shadows of pilings
under the pier. And like a small skiff tied up
in the harbor overnight, she'll figure a way out
of this one too, and in the morning be gone.

LEAVING NEW YORK CITY

Walking uptown after work, standing in a crowd
on the corner—the extreme West Side near the highway,
or a little further downtown,
where ten years ago the towers came down—

I was waiting at a crosswalk for the light to change,
when I caught sight of a silver jetliner
lumbering windward over the lucid stacks of Midtown.
As I watched it ascend at an awkward angle,

sunlight flashing off its fuselage, it got stuck
in a moment in my memory—like a photograph
embedded in a film—and for a minute or two,
as if in a trance, I realized

I wasn't breathing anymore or my heart beating.
Sometimes it happens—you die like this, almost
invisible, an outline in chalk,
pedestrians looking down at their phones

while managing politely to step over or around you.
When I lived in New York, I always wanted to leave—
then, after being away awhile, burned to get back
to the maw of city streets, the din of traffic's

exhaustive rush to nowhere.
But at this moment I thought I was gone for good,
and might have tarried there awhile, as one would have,
say, in the late 19th Century, with cane and top hat,

marveling at the progress of industry,
brick and ironwork façades
of new buildings going up almost overnight—
the invasion of electricity and streetcars dialing up

and driving the pace in which civilization's cranked
toward the future.
As the light changed, and I began to shuffle forward,
head-on into the reflection of sunlight on steel, this

contemporaneous now,
I took a noisy swallow of air and woke up
to the familiar claw of desire—the insatiable ache for
the truth I wanted but knew I'd never have.

WHAT WILL BECOME OF THEM, THIS HAPPY

family: mom, dad, brother and sister?
Will the children grow up and scatter
to opposite corners of the map?
Will they migrate north and south,

one to the city, another deeper into the North
Woods? Will the goofy, blond-headed boy
put on weight and be content to live alone
in a small house at the edge of town—

drawing cartoons, playing video games,
riding his snowmobile and collecting
guns? What will be his final chapter?
Will it end with a period, question mark,

ellipses or exclamation point in bold type?
And what about his sister, who showed
so much promise? Will she follow
her bliss to Broadway—or, after a variety

of dead-end relationships, settle in town
as a hairdresser, marry a quiet mechanic
with whom she'll have an only child?
Will she come to terms, to Jesus, to the end

of her rope? Will her story be an epic,
a continuing saga, and have a sequel?
And what about mom—where will she go?
Will she move back to New York City

after the divorce, and start dating again
the businessman whose proposal she spurned,
twenty years earlier, to marry instead
the manic-depressive poet? Will she return

to her old neighborhood in Brooklyn,
where she lived quietly alone with her cat,
building a career in interior design before
the poet swept her off her feet? Where

will her new life lead? Back to friends
she abandoned after falling in love, having
children and losing herself completely in
the management of the household

and selfless support of her husband's erratic
career? What about this poet—the one called
husband, dad—where will he go from here?
Back to the monastery of his mind,

the one he flirted with in his youth and later
obsessed over, when he should have been
pursuing a practical career, earning a
pension and building his IRA?

Will he be let go from the company he served
loyally? Will he drift around awhile,
from hack job to hack job, falling in finally
with a blonde, chain-smoking divorcé

from the Carrabassett Valley—
who will loan him a cabin in the woods,
in which to live and anguish over his long,
rambling, incoherent and unfinished memoir?

TRANQUILITY BASE

You've heard enough about our planet—now,
tell us something about yours.
Are there menacing blue clouds
riveted to an acetylene sky,
under which you scramble on spring mornings
to avoid the confetti of gunfire?
How far are your stars—
and are there other worlds in your science
about which you sing and suppress?
Who are your ladies and what
are your gentlemen?
Are there theaters in your cities
blasting forth a wish of undeleted applause?
Is there language in your touch?
Can you extend your tongue far enough to taste
the sweet loaf of derision?
Are there copious opposites where you live
or only one *One*?
What color is your sun,
and does it stick to the horizon at noon
like a wet sponge to a window?
Do you watch a moon or two rise
through one long sentence of razor wire—
and are you wounded with their every ascent?
Does everyone have a name,
and do you call for each other
across crepuscular fields—your replies faint
as fragrant, sexual innuendoes?
Are your women supple and exotic?
Are your men carved from the rock on which
your civilization teeters
as they guard the gates of home
with 40-pound spears?
Do your children chase fireflies on fairy tale
nights, ten thousand miles

from the roil of war?
Is there war on your planet—or is it tranquil,
languid and lazy as a dream?

NOTES

"Bird Hunting" is dedicated to the memory of my father.

"Long Distance" is for Ted Somogyi.

"Return to the Place of a Poem" is dedicated to the memory of Shelley Hoffman.

"Recorded History: Avon Cemetery; Central Iowa, 1998" is based on conversations with my grandfather who grew up on a farm southeast of Des Moines, Iowa, and is for Donald Hall.

"Morning Poem" is for Mary Rehak.

"Never Coming Home" is dedicated to the memory of those who lost their lives in the attacks of 9/11.

"Tranquility Base" is inspired by Czeslaw Miloz's poem "Tidings."

ABOUT THE AUTHOR

Christopher Seid holds an MFA from Vermont College and has published one previous book of poems, *Prayers to the Other Life*, which won the Marianne Moore Poetry Prize. Born and raised in Iowa, he has lived in Brooklyn, Boston, California—and various points in between. For the past 12 years he has made his home in Yarmouth, Maine, with his two children. He works as a freelance writer and serves on the board of the Telling Room, a nonprofit writing center for children and young adults in Portland, Maine.

Printed in the United States of America

Main
9
15.95

PORTLAND PUBLIC LIBRARY SYSTEM
5 MONUMENT SQUARE
PORTLAND, ME 04101

WITHDRAWN

CPSIA information can be obtained at www.ICGtesting.com
Printed in the USA
BVOW02s0103160415

396354BV00001B/23/P

9 781421 837239